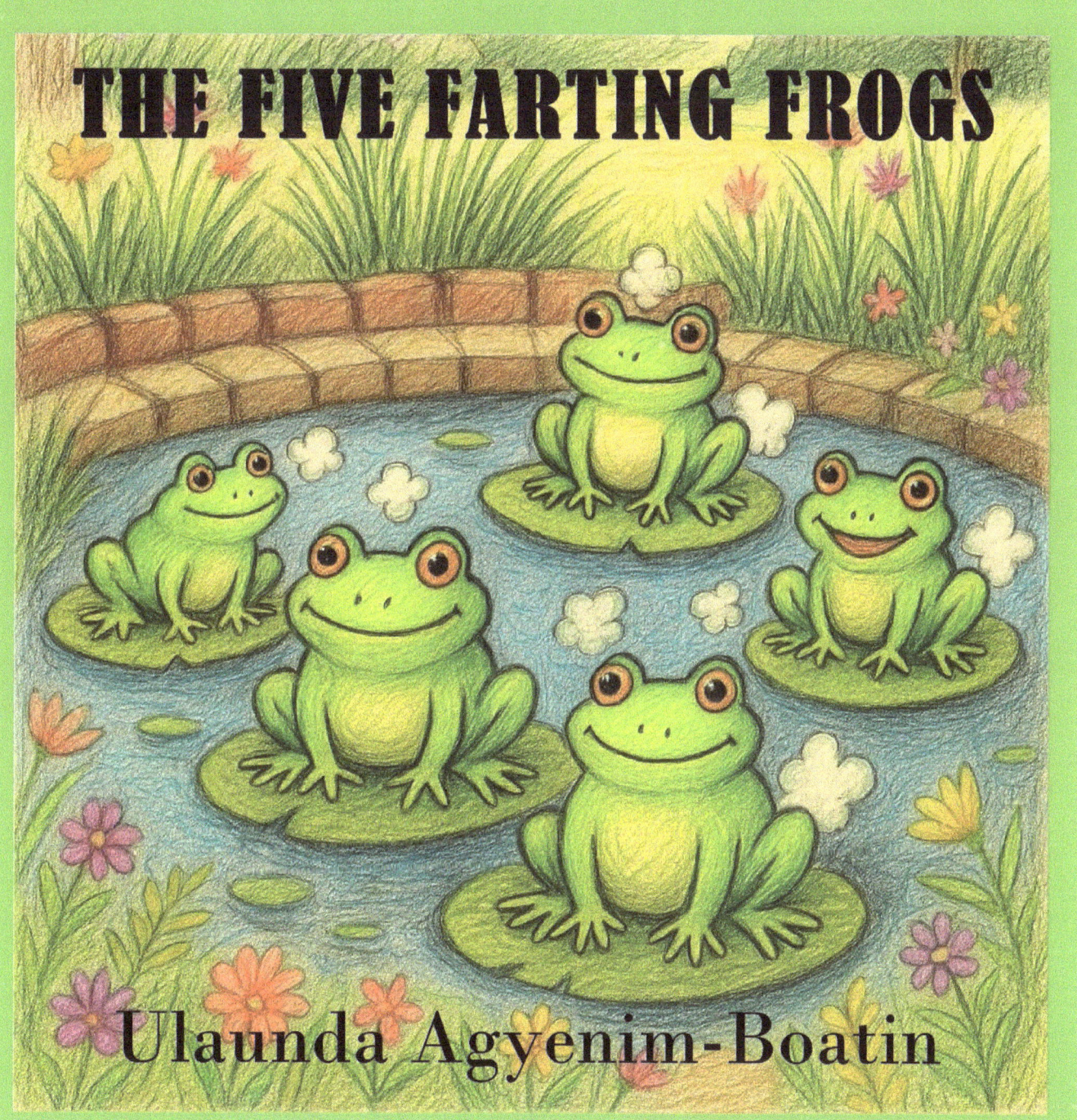

INTRODUCTION

The Five Farting Frogs is a very humorous and whimsical children's book that follows five frogs. Each one has its own distinct personality and a mischievous farting habit, and they have a blast doing it.

Through their amusing escapades, each one of the frogs embraces their individuality.

The charming story highlights each frog's unique reason for farting. It is complemented by lively illustrations, making it an entertaining read for young children while gently teaching them that farting is a natural part of life. However, when you fart, it is polite to say, "Excuse me."

THE FIVE FARTING FROGS

By Ulaunda Agyenim-Boatin

Illustrations: Isaac Brown III

Once in a pond, not far from the bay, lived five funny frogs.

On a beautiful day, they were leaping and laughing.

But oh! What a noise each of them made!

4

Fizzle was first and the smallest of all. Her toots were so tiny, like bubbles.

She would hiccup and giggle with delight while sending small bubbles up into the night.

Bloop comes next, a jolly green fellow whose farts were like a tuba as well as long and loud, but mellow.

He would hop in the water with a giant toot while the duckling would giggle and paddle away.

Tooty was next.

He thought it was cool to fart while he was in the pond.

He would always say, "It is better out than in," while puffed with pride.

Ziggy-Ziggy was the fourth frog who liked to leap.

He loved to zip through the reels and jump over the logs.

Whenever he landed, he would let out a loud Pow-Pow!

The last frog was Grumble.

Grumble hardly ever spoke, but his farts were so mighty and strong, like a mighty shack with a rumble and roar.

He let one out from his pad like a storm that would knock your feet off the ground.

The five frogs were all silly and bold. They expressed themselves in their own unique way through their farts.

Now that they have farted, they feel happy and free.

ACKNOWLEDMENTS

This book would not exist without God, for which I am grateful.

I want to express a heartfelt acknowledgment to the memory of my late husband, Kwabena Agyenim-Boatin, whom I am very grateful for meeting in college. I also learned from him.

Additionally, thanks to Anelda Attaway and the whole Jazzy Kitty Publications team for publishing it and helping to realize my vision through illustrations.

Gwen Ishmael and her daughter Stephanie deserve special recognition for their motivation, inspiration, encouragement, and support.

DEDICATIONS

This heartfelt dedication beautifully expresses my wish for children worldwide to find joy and laughter in every moment, inspiring a sense of happiness and positivity.

A special acknowledgment to Poet Ebo, who shared with me the importance of writing. Her encouragement and support helped me with my creativity, expression, and confidence to write this book.

To all of you: May my words reflect a generous spirit aimed at spreading joy and inspiring others through my writing.

ABOUT THE AUTHOR

Ulaunda Agyenim-Boatin was born and raised in Philadelphia, Pennsylvania. She graduated from high school, earning her diploma in 1978. Ulaunda continued her studies at Capella University, where she graduated with a Master of Science degree in Education.

Ulaunda is a proud mother of two children and the cherished grandmother of five. She is also a great-grandmother to two beautiful grandchildren.

THE FIVE FARTING FROGS

Author Ulaunda Agyenim-Boatin

Illustrations: Isaac Brown III

Editor: Anelda Attaway

Published by Jazzy Kitty Publications, Wilmington, DE

Copyright © 2025 Ulaunda Agyenim-Boatin

ISBN 978-1-965381-14-4

Library of Congress Control Number 2025918093

All rights are explicitly reserved worldwide. This book is protected under the copyright laws of the United States of America. This book may not be copied or reprinted for commercial profit or net income. The purpose of short quotations or occasional page copying for personal or group study is permitted and promoted. Permission to copy will be freely granted upon request for Worldwide Distribution and printed and published in the United States of America. Created Jazzy Kitty Greetings Marketing & Publishing, LLC dba Jazzy Kitty Publications, is utilizing Microsoft Publishing, Photoshop, and BookCoverly Software.

www.ingramcontent.com/pod-product-compliance
Lightning Source LLC
Chambersburg PA
CBHW061350010526
44107CB00011B/896